NK 12/13

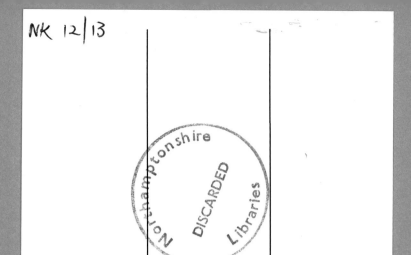

PEOPLE IN HISTORY

Popcorn

Elizabeth I

Stephen White-Thomson

WAYLAND

Explore the world with **Popcorn -** your complete first non-fiction library.

Look out for more titles in the Popcorn range. All books have the same format of simple text and striking images. Text is carefully matched to the pictures to help readers to identify and understand key vocabulary. www.waylandbooks.co.uk/popcorn

First published in 2013 by Wayland
Copyright © Wayland 2013

Wayland
Hachette Children's Books
338 Euston Road
London NW1 3BH

Wayland Australia
Level 17/207 Kent Street
Sydney NSW 2000

Produced for Wayland by
White-Thomson Publishing Ltd
www.wtpub.co.uk
+44 (0)843 208 7460

Editor: Stephen White-Thomson
Designer: Clare Nicholas
Picture researcher: Stephen White-Thomson
Series consultant: Kate Ruttle
Design concept: Paul Cherrill

A catalogue for this title is available from the British Library

952'.055'092-dc23

978 0 7502 7918 5

10 9 8

William Shakespeare

Picture/illustration credits:
akg-images: 10; Bridgeman Art Library: 4, 11, 14; Bull, Peter: illustration 23; Corbis: Joel W. Rogers 17, Hoberman Collection 19, Angelo Hornak 21; Shutterstock.com: Georgios Kollidas imprint and 22, C.J. Williamson 12, Kamira 15(b), David Hughes 15(t); Wikimedia: cover, title page, 5, 6 (both), 7, 8, 9, 12-13, 16, 20, 22.

Every effort has been made to clear copyright. Should there be any inadvertent omission, please apply to the publisher for rectification.

# Contents

Elizabeth's England

The Tudors were a family who ruled England about 500 years ago. They ruled England for around 120 years. Elizabeth was the last of the Tudors.

This painting shows the clothes that different people wore when Elizabeth was queen.

Mercatorum vxores.   Nobiles mulieres Anglia

When Elizabeth was queen there were a few people who were rich and powerful. Most people were poor and lived in the country. Many worked on farms.

This portrait of Elizabeth shows her beautiful clothes.

Early life

Princess Elizabeth was born in 1533. She was the daughter of King Henry VIII and Queen Anne Boleyn. Her mother was beheaded when Elizabeth was only two years old.

Elizabeth's parents, Henry VIII and Anne Boleyn.

When Henry VIII died in 1547, Elizabeth's half brother became King Edward VI. He died when he was only 15. Elizabeth's half sister became Queen Mary I.

This painting shows King Henry with his children, Mary, Edward and Elizabeth.

Mary

Edward

Elizabeth

Elizabeth becomes queen

Queen Mary was unpopular. Some people wanted to make Elizabeth their queen. Mary locked Elizabeth in the Tower of London to keep her out of the way.

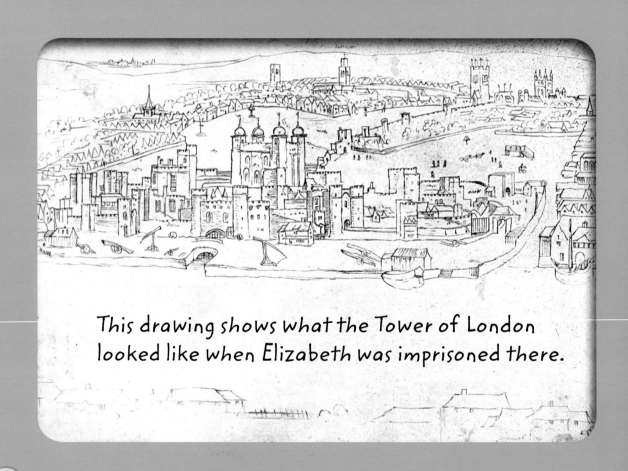

This drawing shows what the Tower of London looked like when Elizabeth was imprisoned there.

Mary died in 1558 and Elizabeth became queen. At her coronation she was given a ring which she wore for the rest of her life.

Elizabeth was 25 when she became queen.

Travelling around

Elizabeth enjoyed travelling around the country so that people could see her. She dressed in beautiful clothes that were covered in jewels so she looked powerful.

Elizabeth is carried through a crowd in London.

When Elizabeth visited places in
the countryside, she travelled with
lots of guards to keep her safe.
Her hosts wanted her to be happy.
They gave feasts to welcome her.

Elizabeth arrives in a carriage
at Nonsuch Palace in Surrey.

Tudor houses

Lots of houses built in Elizabeth's reign are still used today. Some were made out of wood. Even a farmer's house took 30 trees to build!

Many Tudor houses were built using wooden frames that were painted black.

Elizabeth always stayed in grand houses. She liked to stay in Hatfield House where she sometimes lived when she was a child.

You can visit Hatfield House today.

Elizabeth was at Hatfield House when she heard she was to be queen!

Entertaining the queen

Elizabeth had many hobbies. As well as riding, she played musical instruments, enjoyed dancing and wrote poetry. She was very clever.

When she was 11, Elizabeth could speak six languages.

This painting shows Elizabeth playing the lute.

Elizabeth liked the plays that William Shakespeare wrote. They were performed in the Globe Theatre in London. In 1997, the theatre was rebuilt as it looked in Elizabeth's time.

Actors perform a Shakespeare play in the Globe Theatre.

Famous explorers

During Elizabeth's reign, sailors set out to explore unknown parts of the world. Walter Raleigh was a famous explorer. Elizabeth made him Sir Walter.

Walter Raleigh brought back the potato plant from America.

A painting of Sir Walter Raleigh.

Francis Drake sailed round the world in his ship the *Golden Hinde* from 1577 to 1580. He attacked Spanish ships and returned to England with lots of treasure for the queen.

This is what the *Golden Hinde* looked like.

The Spanish Armada

In 1588, a huge fleet, or 'armada', of Spanish ships sailed to England. It had been sent by the King of Spain, Philip II, to invade England.

A painting of the Spanish Armada.

The smaller English fleet won the battle in the English Channel. They sent little fireships into the Spanish fleet and set fire to many of the big ships.

This gold coin shows one of Elizabeth's ships.

Queen of Hearts

Elizabeth never married. There were plenty of men who wanted to marry her, but she said she was married to England. She wanted to pay attention to making England a strong country.

Elizabeth nearly married the handsome Robert Dudley, Earl of Leicester.

Elizabeth died in 1603. She had been queen for 45 years. She was loved by her people who called her 'Good Queen Bess'.

Elizabeth's tomb is in Westminster Abbey in London.

After Elizabeth, James VI of Scotland became King James I of England as well.

 # Quiz!

Here are some of the important men in Elizabeth's life. Look through the book again and see if you can link the names of the men in the labels with the right paintings.

a.
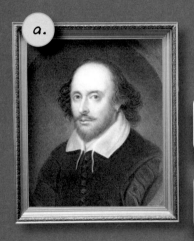

b.

1. Henry VIII
- her father

2. Robert Dudley
- a nobleman

3. Sir Walter Raleigh
- an explorer

4. William Shakespeare
- wrote plays

c.

d.

Make a Tudor knot garden

You will need:
• foil or plastic tray
• kitchen sponge cloth
• cress seeds

Rich Tudors kept beautiful gardens. They grew herbs in them to flavour their food.

1. Design your knot garden on a piece of paper the same size as your kitchen sponge cloth.

2. Ask an adult to help you cut the sponge to make the same pattern as you made on the paper. Put it in the tray and soak with water.

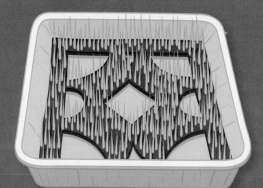

3. Sprinkle the sponge area with cress seeds and leave on a windowsill to grow. Gently water the seeds until you have your garden!

Glossary

beheaded to have your head cut off

carriage something that is pulled by horses for people to travel in

coronation when someone is made a king or queen

feast a special big meal for many people

fleet a lot of ships all sailing close together

hobbies things you do for fun in your spare time

hosts people who welcome and entertain guests at home or elsewhere

imprisoned kept locked up

invade to go into another country to take it over

lute a musical instrument that looks and sounds a bit like a guitar

tomb a place where dead bodies are buried

treasure gold, silver and jewels

unpopular not liked

Index

EXPLORE THE WORLD WITH THE POPCORN NON-FICTION LIBRARY!

- Develops children's knowledge and understanding of the world by covering a wide range of topics in a fun, colourful and engaging way
- Simple sentence structure builds readers' confidence
- Text checked by an experienced literacy consultant and primary deputy-head teacher
- Closely matched pictures and text enable children to decode words
- Includes a cross-curricular activity in the back of each book

FREE DOWNLOADS!

- Written by an experienced teacher
- Learning objectives clearly marked
- Provides information on where the books fit into the curriculum
- Photocopiable so pupils can take them home

www.waylandbooks.co.uk/downloads